RUMI

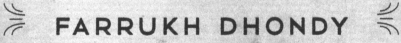

A NEW TRANSLATION
OF SELECTED
POEMS

Translated and with an Introduction by

FARRUKH DHONDY

ARCADE PUBLISHING · NEW YORK

First Arcade Paperback Edition 2017

First published in India by HarperCollins Publishers India

Arcade Publishing books may be purchased in bulk at special
discounts for sales promotion, corporate gifts, fund-raising, or
educational purposes. Special editions can also be created to
specifications. For details, contact the Special Sales Department,
Arcade Publishing, 307 West 36th Street, 11th Floor, New York, NY
10018 or arcade@skyhorsepublishing.com.

Arcade Publishing® is a registered trademark of Skyhorse
Publishing, Inc.®, a Delaware corporation.

Visit our website at www.arcadepub.com.

10 9 8 7 6 5 4 3

Library of Congress Cataloging-in-Publication Data is available
on file.

Cover illustration: iStockphoto

Print ISBN: 978-1-62872-697-8
Ebook ISBN: 978-1-61145-920-3

Printed in the United States of America

To Mala

Contents

Rumi, Sufism and the Modern World

This can't be a literary or historical introduction to Sufism, nor an adequate biography of Rumi, or even just a foreword to a clutch of poems I've translated.

This is intended partly as all of these, and as a contention that in our times the identification of Sufism as the enduring interpretation of Islam is a political duty.

Sufism is mystical, philosophical and aspirational Islam with deep roots in the history of nearly half the world. It has a vital role to play in our times, when other interpretations of Islam openly challenge and terrorize the East and the West. Even though, as a culture of poets, philosophers and savants, Sufism has never had a political center, it is time it asserted its dominant voice and manifested its popularity in the Muslim world.

The great work of Jalal ad-Din Rumi, the *Mathnawi*, has been referred to as the "Koran in Persian," and it stands in direct contrast to the interpretations of Islam which give rise to terrorism and to ideologies of political dominance.

Sufism and juridical, "literal" Islam, have been in conflict since the martyrdom of Hazrat Ali. Their differences have burst into war and dissension in several parts of the Islamic world. Today, the world sees a violent assertion of what its followers call "political Islam." However, as Edmund Burke said, "the crickets may be the loudest, but are not the largest creatures in the field," and so Sufism, though not a combative philosophy, has fought its philosophical and eschatological battles within the enclosed polity of the Muslim world, in which young men choose to fly planes into American buildings in New York and subsequently kill three thousand strangers.

The response of the United States is to go to war, and several devastating terrorist incidents and restraining arrests follow. The tendency professing to be the champion of Islam claims responsibility. They are waging a jihad: it is an attack on the values, the democracies and the government policies of the West. The terrorists profess to pose the question: "What kind of a civilization do you want?" The world responds by not recognizing their authority to question, and by questioning back.

What do the terrorists, who act in the name of Islam, want? There is no clear answer.

Books are published and TV programs are aired. These have come to the not-so-remarkable conclusion that there are conflicting trends in Islam between the fundamentalists and what the West calls "the moderates." The governments of the West—Europe and the USA—repeatedly assert that they are not anti-Islamic or anti-Muslim, though within the Muslim world the suspicion remains that there indeed is a clash of civilizations.

Sufi Islam has participated neither in the dissension nor in the debate. From the time of the Prophet, the Sufi tradition, without that name, has asserted itself as the truth, but, by its nature cannot see itself as a political formation.

Contemporary translations of the works of Rumi—the greatest single work of Sufism in history—have not interpreted his work as a seminal document asserting the "moderation" of Islam, nor as a counterbalance to the world-negating tendencies of the terrorists. A reading of Rumi's work today and its dissemination can go towards demonstrating to those within the Muslim world and those outside it the object of the quest of Sufi Islam.

However, the translations that have become popular—through international publications and the internet—have treated his work as "hippy freakishness," the pretentious and reader-flattering "philosophy" of the likes of Kahlil Gibran, or prosaic titbits to flatter the fans of pop divas who want to turn their attention to acclaimed poetry.

A transliteration of Rumi's work should have a more serious intention in our times. The philosophical stance he fought for in the thirteenth century AD and the survival of the Sufi tradition, extended and developed by him, are vital to our world.

Jalal ad-Din, the poet and savant we know as Rumi,

acquired his second name from the Arabic word *rum*, for Rome. He wasn't born with the honorific that became his name and only acquired it when traveling with his father who was exiled, or chose exile, from their native town of Balkh, and settled finally in Konya, now in western Turkey. The west of Turkey, though not ruled from Constantinople at the time, was still known as part of the Eastern Roman Empire, the territory of Rome.

Rumi was born in 1207 and died in 1273 AD. He was an older contemporary of Saint Thomas Aquinas, who was born in 1225 and died in 1274 in Florentine, Italy. The fact is significant, as Aquinas is to the Catholic world the most prestigious interpreter of Jesus' gospel, and Rumi's work, the *Mathnawi* is, as I noted earlier, referred to as the Koran in verse. The fact that both Aquinas and Rumi found a following and such great claims were made for each would indicate that the theologies of the thirteenth century, Christian and Muslim, were ready for or receptive to reformation and reformulation. This was at a time when these faiths were at war with each other. The Crusades, the European–Christian endeavor to regain the Holy Land from Islam, began in the eleventh century and ended only two centuries later.

From the point of view of the Muslims who had conquered and converted Persia, parts of Central Asia, most of the Middle East, North Africa and southern Spain, the Crusades became a battle for ownership of the Holy Land and, symbolically, for religious survival.

In the same century, 1220 AD onwards, came the assault from the east and the north, when the Mongol chieftain Temujin proclaimed himself Genghis Khan and, with his fast-moving cavalry, devastated and looted the Muslim kingdoms of Central Asia and Iran.

Rumi lived in troubled times and his boyhood was far from peaceful. His father, Baha ud-Din Muhammad ibn al-Husain al-Kahtib al-Baqri, a scholar, philosopher and lecturer whose tribulations were as extensive as his name, was forced to leave Balkh, an exile in the cause of belief. Baha ud-Din was a Sufi and follower of the eleventh-century Sufi savant Ghazali. He was known among his followers as Sultan al-Ulama, the "king of scholars." As such, in Balkh, he came up against the more orthodox followers of scholastic Islam, whom he and Ghazali characterized as decadent and hollow jurists rather than Muslims. His Sufi faction was defeated in the court of Balkh, or it may have been that Baha ud-Din, content in his certainties, was indifferent to the politics of Islamic courts and left of his own accord.

His grandson and Rumi's son, Sultan Walad, records in the annals of the family that Baha was offended by the people of Balkh and received a divine message that enjoined him to leave the city, on which God's punishment was about to fall.

The exact dates and circumstances of his exile and travels are still disputed by chroniclers, but it is thought that Baha ud-Din left Balkh with his family somewhere between 1213 and 1220 AD and went to Nishapur. Sure enough, the vengeance of God fell upon Balkh in the shape of the Mongol armies under Genghis Khan.

Baha ud-Din and his son traveled to Baghdad and thence to Mecca and Syria.

In his eighteenth year, Jalal ad-Din went with his father to Erzincan and Larinda. In this town, a marriage was arranged for the young Jalal ad-Din, and a year later Sultan Walad was born. And yet Baha ud-Din was unsettled.

We may assume he traveled because he was offered posts of scholarship in different cities—just like a modern-day visiting lecturer—by the sultans and governors of those places. The ruler of Erzincan, Fakhr-ud-din Bahram Shah, a patron of learning, invited Baha to his kingdom to deliver discourses. After four years in Erzincan, the Seljuq Sultan of Konya, persuaded by the fame of Baha ud-Din, invited him to settle as his intellectual-in-residence. Baha accepted the invitation and, at the age of twenty-two, Jalal ad-Din settled in Konya.

The mantle of "king of scholars" fell on Jalal ad-Din's twenty-four-year-old shoulders when, two years later, Baha died and the patronage of the sultan, Ala' ud-Din Key-Qobad, was extended and renewed.

Rumi had been born into the tradition and teachings of Ghazali. Known by the magnificent title of Hajat-ul-Islam or the "Proof of Islam," Ghazali was a revivalist and a reformer of Islam. The influence of Greek philosophy, the pre-Christian, Platonic and Aristotelian thought, had penetrated the minds and methods of scholastic Islam, and Ghazali saw this as a negation of the founding spirit of Islam itself.

The origins of Sufism are disputed. Scholars such as Andrew Rippin[1] point to the birth of Sufism as a product of a religious contradiction. By the eighth and ninth centuries, Islam had spread to cultures other than the Arab tribes of the Middle East. It had, most significantly, conquered Persia and subdued the prevalent state religion of Zoroastrianism. The split between Shia and Sunni Islam was already established, with the Shias, predominantly Persian, following the Prophet's son-in-law Ali, who opposed the usurper Muawiyah who had named himself Caliph or successor to the Prophet. Their enmity, though springing from internecine quarrels and murder in the camps and Caliphate of early Islam, could be attributed to a rejection by Ali's followers of the materialistic Islam of Muawiyah and his son Yazid, pretenders to the throne and the tradition.

By the eighth century, according to some scholars, the spiritual traditions of the pre-Islamic Persians began to assert themselves and took the form of a spiritual quest that then sought the legitimacy of Islam. It needed this

---

1. Andrew Rippin, *Muslims: Their Religious Beliefs and Practices* (London: Routledge, 1990).

legitimacy, as otherwise it would be seen as a heresy and eradicated. The early Sufis had to demonstrate with reference to Koranic text that "Islam as a religion contained within it a spiritual-ascetic tendency from the very beginning . . . To suggest that Islamic mysticism is, in fact, a borrowing from outside raises the spectre of denial of the intrinsically spiritual nature of Islam and thence the spiritual nature of Muslims themselves."[2]

This was a real danger. As it is, the Shias of Persia had inherited the Zoroastrian structures of a priestly caste, the dasturs, who now exist in the form of ayatollahs as separate from the lay Muslim, a tradition that doesn't exist in Sunni Islam. The Shias still celebrate the Zoroastrian Navroz (Nowruz) or New Year on March 21, the vernal equinox prescribed by Persian astronomers. If their mystical inclinations owed anything to the old religion, they had to find legitimacy with the current power.

Sufis quote the suras of the Koran as evidence of the origin of their faith.

Sura 24:35:

> Allah is the Light of Heaven and earth! . . . A glittering star kindled from a blessed olive tree which neither Eastern nor Western, whose oil will

---

2. Rippin, *Muslims, Their Religious Beliefs and Practices.*

almost glow though the fire has never touched it.
Light upon Light, Allah guides anyone he wishes
to his light.

And then again in sura 50:6,

We (Allah) are nearer to him (man) than his
jugular vein.

Undoubtedly these and other verses of the Koran can be
interpreted as the Sufis do, contending that man is a part
of God and vice versa, and to Him he shall return, that
the essence is effulgence, the "light upon light." Added
to the specific suras is the Sufi conviction that the Koran
has an outward and an inward meaning. They state that
Sufi thought or *"tasawwuf* is the esoteric or inward (*batin*)
aspect of Islam."[3]

Throughout the history of Islam, there have been
scholars from various schools who have opposed Sufism.
Some, such as the Wahabi, go so far as to regard Sufism
as an outright heresy. Sufi beliefs have been argued
over by these scholars, "their practices condemned, their
dervishes ridiculed and occasionally executed, and their
sheikhs castigated."[4] And yet vast numbers of Muslims

---

3 Titus Berckhardt, *An Introduction to Sufism* (Wellingborough:
Aquarian Press, 1990).

4. J. Spence Trimingham, *The Sufi Orders in Islam* (Oxford: The
Clarendon Press, 1998).

in the Indian subcontinent, in Iran and all over the non-Arab Muslim world are adherents of or sympathetic to this spiritual quest.

Did Sufism use Islam as a cover, a legitimizing insurance policy while pursuing, developing and incorporating beliefs that emanate from Christian mystics, Buddhism and almost certainly from pre-Islamic Zoroastrianism? Many scholars believe this to be true.

Today, Sufism is a living religion within the Islamic tradition and the Ulema. While it diligently professes the fundamental belief of Islam that there is one God and that Muhammad is his last prophet, any scrutiny of its history will yield a wealth of allusions and influences from other religions and beliefs.

Elliot Miller in his definitive book, *Sufism and the Mystical Muslims* (Foreword, 1986) says: "Sufism has always been more open to outside influence than other forms of Islam. In addition to early influences from Christianity, one can find elements of Zoroastrianism, Neoplatonism, Hinduism and other diverse traditions."

One of the historical figures of Sufism, Prince Dara Shikoh (d.1619), the eldest son of Mughal emperor Shah Jahan, was a Sufi of the Qadriyya order. He regarded himself as a devout Muslim and scholar and devoted part of his tragic life to translating Hindu scriptural texts— the Bhagvad Gita and the Upanishads—from Sanskrit to Persian. Dara Shikoh believed the Upanishads to be the "hidden books" to which the Koran refers. He wrote that "they contain the essence of unity and they are secrets which have to be kept hidden." His study of Hindu philosophy led him to believe that Sufism and Advaita Vedanta, the essential philosophy of the Upanishads and the Bhagvad Gita, are the same.

Dara Shikoh's testimony is perhaps the strongest recognition of this common mystical ground—the foundation of the spiritual belief in the oneness of God, the human soul and all the universal manifestations of energy. He was an Indian prince, cruelly executed by his younger brother Aurangzeb, a fundamentalist Muslim who killed him as much to seize the throne as for what he considered his un-Islamic beliefs.

It is probably from the inception or revelation of Islam that the Sufi tradition took upon itself the idealization of the relationship between the master and disciple. Prophet Muhammad had four devoted disciples, among them Salman the Persian, who would have brought Zoroastrian beliefs with him as part of his devotion to the prophet of God, a God recognized equally singly by Zoroastrians as Ahura Mazda (who, according to the twentieth-century Sufi Inayat Khan, contributes the "hu" in the mystic invocation "Allah-hu"). These disciples, like those of Jesus (Issah, in Rumi's texts), imbibed the teachings and went forth to spread them. The master–disciple relationship in Sufism of the sheikh and the murid, the learner, is much closer in spirit and practice to the prescribed relationship of the guru and the chela in Hindu tradition.

The sheikh is not simply the repository of a passed-on wisdom. In him, the murid sees a light that he must acquire through knowledge, through meditation, through the purging of his desires and consciousness, and through his deeds. "Light upon light!" And the Sufi desires to become a part of "it" through the realization that he always was.

For other orders, acceptance of the five pillars of Islam, obedience of the Sharia and in some cases ritual observance, such as purdah or hijab, are necessary and sufficient practices to include one as a Muslim. For the Sufi these are the minimal garb of the Muslim, the outer and even hollow, unfulfilling forms. The essence of Sufi devotion is the spiritual awakening, the realization, the cleansing, the enlightenment, the oneness—the light. All ritual or practice, which may take the form of whirling dances, of subservience, of devotion to a master; all learning, all association with a master must lead to That.

In the pronouncements of Sufi masters, whatever the apologists and missionaries of fundamentalist and scholastic Islam may say, there are the truths and epiphanies of other mystical religions. Sufism is in truth a universal religion of the spirit which adopted the disciplines of Islam and used its dynamism to disseminate itself. In essence Sufism is, as Advaita Vedanta is, monist and pantheistic. Within the discipline and the revelation of Islam, in which it has chosen to reside and has developed and been disseminated, it cannot adopt the pantheism that gives deities several forms and names and worships them in temples with altars and graven images, but it embraces all forms of devotion.

Ibn 'Arabi, a Sufi mystic of the same century as Rumi, reviled as a heretic by some and honored as a supreme master by others, says:

> My heart has become capable of every form: it is
> a pasture for gazelles and a convent for Christians,
> and a temple for idols and the pilgrims to the
> Ka'ba and the tables of Torah, and the book of the
> Koran. I follow the religion of Love: whatever way
> Love's camels take, that is my religion and faith.

There is, in the Sufi spiritual vocabulary, the lover Laila who literally stands for "night" but is divine reality. She is a metaphor and in Sufi pronouncements takes the form of an illusory deity: "Seekest thou Laila, when she is manifest within thee? Thou deemest her to be other, but she is not other than thou."[5]

The quest is all. No orthodoxy or doctrine of the jurists ought to stand in its way. Mahmud Shabistari in his work

---

5. Muhammad al-Harraq d. 1845.

Gulshan-i Raz (*The Mystic Rose Garden*) declares: "What is a mosque, what is a synagogue, what is a fire-temple? 'I' and 'you' are the veils the devil casts between them. But lift the veils and with them disappears the bonds of sects and creeds that imprison us."

At various times and through the realizations and teachings of various masters, Sufism has declared its debt to creeds and religions other than Islam and sought out and celebrated the common human spiritual quest.

*

Early Islam, rooted in a mystical act of revelation to the Prophet, was nevertheless a new discipline to the polytheistic and pagan tribes of Arabia, its first adherents. In its rapid expansion through military conquest, it became the ideologically orienting force of a new and dynamic nation. Its geographical expansion brought it into contact with other nations, creeds and beliefs, which it sought by persuasion or force to convert. The militaristic, strategic and political considerations of conquest and the governance of the converted; the hubris of armies fired by the new messianic ideology of conquest; the material wealth that was suddenly at the disposal of men from a nomadic and sparse ancestry and tradition overtook and obscured the possible spiritual interpretations of Islam. Its disciplinary and juridical aspects came to the fore in these years.

Perhaps Ali and his predominantly Shia followers, recent converts from decadent Zoroastrianism, sowed the seeds of the quest. Sufism became the interpretation that rushed in to fill the spiritual vacuum of early Islam.

What is indisputable is that the Sufis and their mystical interpretation of Islam do not see Islam as a qualifying extension of the Judeo-Christian monotheistic tradition. Their beliefs are closer to pantheistic and monist Vedanta and also Buddhism. They looked East.[6]

Sufis to this day continue to claim that they are the real Muslims and that the Koran and the Hadith—the acts and sayings of the Prophet—have sanctified their belief and the legitimacy of their yearning. Their opponents within Islam characterize them as heretics and *kafirs*, "unbelievers." They in their turn, when matters come to a head, declare that the Wahabi and so-called fundamentalists are Muslims only by their own assertion and by political fact.

The pronounced identification of Sufism with Advaita Vedanta or with Buddhism is not uncommon in the Indian subcontinent but is not a generally accepted Sufi tenet because there is no central universal Sufi authority and

---

6. To simplify several thousand years of religion and philosophy: Monotheism believes there is only one God, an unknowable quantity from whom we are separated, and Monism believes that there is only one reality of which we are a part and with which we can ultimately be united—the same substance, a drop separated from an ocean by the veil of consciousness.

there has been no politicization of this spiritualist Islamic tendency. Wahabism, in contrast, has since the 1920s been adopted as the religion of the Saudi Arabian state and has recruited adherents wherever petro-dollars can buy, or spread, influence.

After the terrorist declaration of 9/11, various Muslim voices have been raised in opposition to this act of mass murder. A world united by television and the internet wants to know who has declared war on whom and why. Islam has, as never before, been challenged to declare to a globalized world its spiritual, political, military, economic and social objectives.

The arguments for and against the use of terror, as indeed the arguments deployed by Western foreign policy apologists and their opponents, are outside the scope of an introduction to a book of translated verse. Suffice it to say, "moderate" Islam has not found, has not been bold enough, or has not been given the platform to express its profound, theologically argued and absolute Islamic opposition to the heretical faction of wanton murder.

The several orders of Islam that disdain to overtly call themselves Sufi, because the label carries connotations of pollution from the pure tradition, are today the potential proponents of a great world religion whose name has been hijacked by political heretics.

The Sufi tradition has lived and flourished within Islam from the time of Salman, the Persian apostle of the Prophet, through the wars and martyrdom of Ali, through the conquests and annexations of lands and traditions by Islam and the yearnings and evolution of spiritual thought, to today. Fourteen hundred years of these conflicting traditions and the orders they generated have brought no resolution. There was in the past no urgent or terminal need for a resolution. Sufi Islam developed from the time of Ali in parallel to the literal, juridical, materialist, rationalist Islam that Ghazali, the Hujjat al-Islam, (translated as the "Argument" or the "Proof" or the "Word" of Islam), resolved through his genius, the yearnings of the spirit of Muslims with the ritualistic religion that prevailed.

Ghazali's works and pronunciations have been subsequently seen as a metaphysically diplomatic triumph, amalgamating the obligations of action and belief of prescriptive Islam with a spiritual dimension and goal for the believer, as part of Sufi Islam.

Baha ud-Din, Rumi's father, couldn't have been aware of the cautious view of future historians. He saw Ghazali as a master and a revolutionary within the tradition of which he was a student. He embraced the Sufi premise, even though he remained an exponent and philosophical advisor to the court of Balkh.

Though Ghazali is historically credited with reconciling juridical Islam with the Sufi tendencies, earning for himself the title of supreme interpreter, his admirer and direct disciple, Baha ud-Din, came into sharp conflict with the jurists and scholars of the court.

By 1208, when Rumi was one year old, Baha was publicly challenging the rationalists, who interpreted the Koran and the Hadith through methods derived from the Platonic tradition. He maintained, following Ghazali's teachings and interpretations, that there was another way. Baha was engaged in an open debate in the royal court of King Muhammad, the shah of Khwarezm, for a fresh interpretation of the precepts of Islam.

He singled out as a debating opponent and made an enemy of the king's tutor and courtier, an eminent philosopher called Fakhruddin Razi.

It may have been Razi who engineered Baha's downfall, withdrawal and exile from Balkh, which eventually led to the rise of his son Rumi at Konya.

In all his verse, Rumi exhibits and acknowledges his debt to Ghazali and to another poet of the twelfth century. In Book III of the *Mathnawi*, Rumi retells a story of the men of Hind, who are led to an elephant in a darkened environment with only their sense of touch with which to feel and define it. The first character in the story touches its trunk and thinks the elephant's nature is that of a pipe, another touches its ear and mistakes the elephant for a fan and so on. Before Rumi, the same story was told by both Ghazali and Sana'I, but they made the characters blind, whereas Rumi says they were taken into a place of darkness.

The difference is essential. The darkness is a metaphor for a pagan environment, the pre-enlightened state, and where there is darkness, there can possibly be light, but saving five miracles, those blind men are condemned to their ignorance. Rumi's version, unlike the earlier ones, allows for redemption.

*

The twelfth century saw a renaissance of Sufism all through the Muslim world. The final mystical elevation or epiphany of Rumi himself, in the following century, is said to have been inspired by a question that was put to him by his last mentor and inspiration concerning Bayazid al-Bastami, known as the Sage of Khorassan.

The most important philosopher of Sufism after Ghazali was probably Ibn 'Arabi, who was born in Muslim Spain in Murcia in 1165, forty-two years before Rumi. Ibn 'Arabi studied Islam and its tenets in Seville, and in Cordova he met Averroes, the scholastic Muslim interpreter of Aristotle. Ibn 'Arabi was by now an influential Sufi figure in the world of Islam and traveled through the Muslim territories lecturing and preaching. He settled in Cairo in his forties. Cairo had become at the time a center of intellectual Muslim influence, and 'Arabi came into conflict with the jurists, who condemned him as a heretic and threatened to end his life.

He was indicted and condemned and had to flee Cairo, taking refuge in Mecca. He eventually set out for Anatolia and arriving in Konya, acquired as a disciple Sadr ud-Din al-Qunawi, who, after 'Arabi had moved on from Konya to Damascus, became an associate of the young Rumi and served as his imam during the daily prayers.

It was through Qunawi that the intimate doctrines of 'Arabi were conveyed to Rumi, who acknowledges the debt and, according to some, uses this inheritance and builds the greatest edifice of Sufi Islam from its base.

By the age of thirty-four, Rumi of Konya in Anatolia was a respected teacher of Islam, albeit an opponent of the Jurists and an acknowledged disciple of Ghazali and of his own father. He had a following and a steady stream of disciples and students and led the life of a respected savant. It was then that an incident transformed his life and purpose. He was already deep into an understanding of Sufi thought and insights, but his meeting with one Shams, a mysterious mystic from the town of Tabriz, struck him as an epiphany, as the bolt of lightning and the voice of Issah had struck Saul of Tarsus on the road to Damascus.

The story is told of how Rumi was lecturing his students when a stranger, dressed in a tattered black cloak, came and joined the audience. He sat inconspicuously as the lecture progressed. There was a pile of books kept beside Rumi, and all at once the stranger pointed at the books and asked, "What are those?"

Rumi, probably annoyed at being interrupted, replied with some sarcasm, "The likes of you won't know!" He resumed his lecture, and almost immediately the books caught fire, causing Rumi to shout in consternation, "What's going on? How did this happen?"

Pat came the reply from the stranger: "The likes of you won't know." The stranger walked out as the disciples put out the fire. Rumi followed the stranger and caught up with him in the streets.

All reports of the incident say that the conversation that ensued between the stranger and Rumi was not and could not have been recorded. Rumi invited the stranger to his house, and the two of them remained closeted for forty days in discussion and communion. Again, no record of this debate, which changed Rumi's life unutterably, is available.

The meaning of this parable is feasible of interpretation only in the philosophical context of Sufism. The stranger asks the first question pointing to the books both as mundane objects and as repositories of conceptual, grammatized knowledge. The answer is contemptuous, sarcastic even—only a fool doesn't know what a pile of books is, and it is obvious that the same fool is unlikely to have any acquaintance with the knowledge contained therein. The knowing and not knowing is about knowledge itself. And then the mysterious conflagration and Rumi, perturbed by this event without an apparent cause, an event outside the realm of rational investigation, asks what it is. His question "How did this happen?" or even as we would say colloquially, "What the hell is going on?" to which the stranger answers that it is the professor who "doesn't and can't know." There is more to know than that contained within the books or in pure logic and discourse. Knowledge is mystical, and the spontaneous combustion of the books, works of philosophical reason, is in itself symbolic.

An instinctive evaluation of the meaning and significance of the incident humbled Rumi and impelled him to follow the stranger into the street.

Another story of their first encounter tells us that Shams steps forward in the street as Rumi is passing by on a mule and grabs the mule's bridle. To the astonishment of the students and disciples following Rumi on foot, the stranger addresses a question to Rumi:

"Tell me, was Muhammad the greater servant of God or Bayazid of Bastam?"

Without hesitation Rumi says, 'Muhammad was incomparably the greater."

"Then," replies Shams, "how is it that Muhammad said, 'We have not known thee oh God, as thou rightly shouldst be known,' whereas Bayazid said: 'Glory unto me! How very great is my Glory?'"

On hearing this question Rumi faints.

The words of Bayazid were endowed with the Sufi identification with God, the oneness that is the goal of the quest, whereas the humbler supplication of the Prophet betrayed a distance from Him.

Naturally, Rumi fainted at the very audacity of the perception, and when he recovered he took the mysterious questioner home.

Those same forty days passed in communion.

Rumi emerged from the closeted session a changed man.

The academic, the professor, the lecturer and preacher was no more. The inheritor of his father's title of "king of scholars" was now a disciple of the stranger, Shams-e Tabrizi, the man from the Persian city, who, it is said, had left his native town to travel the world in search of a soul destined for enlightenment.

Had he found such a soul in Rumi? Whether Shams's quest ended with the discovery of Rumi, one does not know, but Jalal ad-Din was transformed entirely. He abandoned lecturing and began a ritual of devotion to his "lover," in whom, as his disciples, family and associates observed, he had discerned some mystical light, power and attraction. Here was the enlightened one, the one who knew, the one who could lead him to that ecstasy and union with the oneness of things that the Sufis call Allah.

Shams remained in Konya with Rumi for, some reports say, seven months, while others claim a longer sojourn of eighteen. He became the object of jealousy of Rumi's disciples whose study and disciplines had been thrown into utter confusion by the arrival of the mystical stranger.

Then just as unaccountably as he had arrived, Shams left, and Rumi, refusing to accept his dereliction, wrote to him in Tabriz and sent emissaries and missives to summon him and tempt him to return. Finally, Rumi sent his son Sultan Walad, and Shams returned with him the following year. Rumi had extracted from his followers and family the confession that their resentment of him had been a supreme error. The promises of acceptance were easily made and just as easily broken. Shams came back into Rumi's life and then, as before, disappeared. One story claims that he was poisoned by Rumi's followers, who regretted his influence on their teacher. They regarded him as the nobility of Russia would regard Rasputin and his mystical influence over their empress. Rumi, it is said, refused to accept that Shams was dead. There was no body and no funeral, no lamentation of the death, just an absence where there had been a presence. He even went to Tabriz, and to several other places, looking for the one who had transformed his consciousness, if indeed there was such a division between the knower and the known.

Had Rumi learned that the absence of the body of Shams was in itself a test? His declarations of the pain of separation, the yearning to have the "beloved" return, are succeeded in his verse by the realization or at least assertion that the spirit of the beloved is one with the spirit of the lover, the "you" is the "I."

And so began the phase of Rumi's life that gave the world his poetic works and earned him the reputation of one of the greatest poets of his tradition. According to his son and biographer, Sultan Walad, the appearance and disappearance of Shams transformed Rumi and took him to a higher stage of Sufi enlightenment. His reasoning and logic and his philosophical discourse were replaced by the manifestations of mystical ecstasy, with dancing and whirling and lyrical pronunciation of longing.

The lyrical impulse, over the next twelve years, translated itself into the composition of the *Diwan-e Shams-e Tabrizi*, a compilation of *ghazals*, or lyrics of love and devotion.

The spell, the ecstasy in this period of Rumi's life, in which the lyrical muse enabled the composition of this extensive work of love, gave way to a quieter synthesis.

Rumi now set out to express in poetry the insights that had unsettled his life and put him on the path to realization and God. He wrote his magnum opus, the *Mathnawi*, in the next twelve years, a book of 25,700 verses, which he dictated to Husam-ud-din Chalapi, his disciple, who had, in a more sober way, replaced Shams in his life and to whom he addressed the work—not with the passion with which Shams had gripped him but with the more philosophical purpose of turning the power of expression to the service of truth.

If the *Mathnawi* is indeed the "Koran in Pahlavi," as

it has been famously labeled, then it conveys that second hidden layer of meaning that the Sufi reads in the encrypted Divine Word. Its message is essentially that of those who went before him, the surrender to the Reality that infuses all things and is beyond them, and at the same time identical with them.

Revelation, an act of grace from the beloved, and the epiphany, are the only paths to the truth. The rest is ritual and duty. Logic and the intellect are shackles whose bonds must be transcended or broken, through sudden realization. The metaphors of intoxication, ecstasy, the sensual grip of love, the swoon, the madness, the dissolution are all expressions of this mystical realization of the state beyond mere reason.

As in the teachings of the Buddha, the *Mathnawi* at times enjoins us to detach ourselves from the world without the Hindu ascetic's disdain for it. It is the path to transformation through which the elements become the servants and slaves of the spirit, pain becomes ecstasy, and the slave becomes one with the master. The *Mathnawi* aims at a music of consciousness, or perhaps even a music beyond consciousness.

Rumi died in 1273. By his own testimony he says his poetic gifts are in the service of love, which is man's connection to God. The *Mathnawi* is, despite its success in our own times as something of a pop phenomenon, essentially the religious text of Sufism. Its constant, relentless use of the concepts, conceits and imagery of the Sufi tradition can be translated into English and into a modern idiom, but without their religious context they are stripped of meaning.

The "love" that Rumi speaks of is not the romantic yearning of a Keats, or the ingredient of some American pop lyric. It is the transcendence of earthly relationships. The "ecstasy" is not orgasm, the "madness" not the dementia of the psychotic; "intoxication" is not that brought about by ethanol or marijuana. The beloved is not the man or woman who obsesses you, but the spirit of the eternal manifest in your guide to God.

The Verses

Selected from the *Mathnawi,
Diwan-e Shams-e,* and
The Discourses

THE WORD

Zuleika had a secret, every word
Or phrase she spoke in secret ways referred

To her beloved Yusuf. If she said,
"The moon is out tonight," she meant instead

To say she loved him. When she said, "Aloe"
Or "Spice" or "bread," her confidantes would know

That it was code for Yusuf; every phrase
A tribute to his beauty and his ways.

You could say, and by now you may have guessed,
That Zuleika lived a life that was obsessed

With Yusuf; she had turned the very gift
Of speech to magic, making meanings drift

And making words say what they never meant.
The blandest phrases turned to sentiment

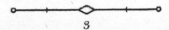

And thoughts and praise of Yusuf. When she cursed
Aloud she meant she wanted time reversed

To once again the hour they last met
When parting made her words turn to regret.

His was the name that every morning burst
From her lips and quenched her every thirst

His name would warm Zuleika in the cold.
And just so, all believers should be told,

That when you seek salvation for your soul
You merge into the ocean of the whole

So lover and beloved are the same
Your Zuleika is merely Yusuf's name

And even though your linguist thinks it odd
All pronouncements are one—the word is "God."

The syllable that permeates all things
Exploding stars and songs the robin sings.

GOING TO MECCA

O pilgrim who visit the Holy Land
I'll show you heaven in a grain of sand

Why traverse deserts, why confront the storm
If within you resides the formless form

Of the Beloved? If he's in your heart
Your pilgrimage has ended where you start.

So, from that garden did you bring a rose?
You saw the house of God, now just suppose

Arriving at a house unoccupied
Will leave the pilgrims' thirst unsatisfied

Remember Hajji wherever you roam
His love will have to make your heart his home.

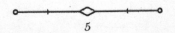

THE WALL

A man could hear beyond a boundary wall
The murmur of a stream. He heard the call

Of running water. Now he longed to quench
His thirst. His hands began to grope and wrench

Loose the wall's topmost stones which he then threw
Into the stream, first one by one, then two

By two—The sound the stones made as they sank
Into the water were like wine—he drank

With gratitude, a sort of substitute
For water of the stream. It was a flute

To his ears, or like thunder bringing rain
To make the desert verdant again

This sound of stones on water wove a spell
That seemed to free the damned from chains of hell

And every stone he dislodged brought him near
The stream of longing. Its message was clear

That God has said prostrate yourself and pray
Break down the walls and barriers so you may

Come to Him as the thirsty come to drink
Beyond the wall, so now approach the brink

Of His eternal stream whose waters speak
And give the seekers nourishment they seek.

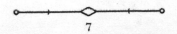

VULTURES

The reason is the human's carrion bird
The questions that it poses are absurd

It feeds on logic, to it ecstasy
Is the main danger and the enemy.

The saintly reason is more like the wings
Of Gabriel who soars above all things

So leave the carrion bird to pick the dead
And soar with me in ecstasy instead.

Come fly with me, I'll take you to a height
Beyond ten thousand vultures in full flight.

RENEWAL FROM THE FALL

Without grinding wheat there can be no bread
No alchemy can turn gold into lead

The surgeon has to use the knife and score
The skin in order to effect a cure

To make a coat the tailor cuts the cloth
A sheep to slaughter makes the festive broth

The builder has to dig the ruins to build
Anything new. The garden's only filled

With roses when the gardener digs the weeds
And turns the soil to plant the new year's seeds

And so my friend, to be remade and whole
Prepare to desecrate your very soul.

THE DANCE

A host of angels dancing in a storm
Define the dance which never takes a form

Who is that bride brought to her love today?
The moon has fetched its gold piled on a tray

Your destiny will shoot its arrows now
The ship will cut the waters with its prow

From shores of the Divine arrives the drift
Of truths that cause the human heart to lift

So when your soul departs you must not mourn
Your soul has merely gone to be reborn

The spirit that vast oceans can't contain
Is evident in every human stain.

LOVERS

Lovers and love live for eternity
All else is borrowed, brother, leave it be

Don't be in thrall to passing shows that fade
Embrace the thing that is of spirit made

Love gives you wings to fly up to that place
Beyond the hundred veils of airy space

To be born you must first renounce each breath
And on the journey turn towards that death

That blinds you to the world and to the "I"
That tells you, you are eternity's sigh.

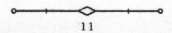

BY HIS WILL

Only by His will do atoms move
The beat of every wing He must approve

No one can explain this and none should try
The infinite can never answer "why?"

Even though we strive to know the "how?"
Through science, before Him we have to bow

And give ourselves, our lives and will to God
With no thought of a blessing or reward

In these our lives, my friend, nor in the next
Does this simple truth leave your mind perplexed?

Then know that contentment is part of bliss
Don't ask for love, and yet accept a kiss.

O Sufi, do not long for paradise
Be content with His love, this earth, these skies.

QUATRAINS

My friend, in friendship as you nearer drew
My faith in love's religion stronger grew
How is it that your creation can see
The worlds you made and still they can't see you?

*

Know only that which makes the unknown known
Before the sands of fleeting life are blown
What you think you've grasped is but a void
The bird in hand is that one which has flown

*

The Muslim and the unbeliever share
This world of joy, this world of shame and care
Beyond, there is a place without Islam
Or disbelief—Come, let me take you there.

GROWING UP

How soon the infant weaned forgets the breast
How soon the fledgling flown forgets the nest

The seed that takes its nurture from the ground
Worships the sun as soon as it has found

The power streaming down from heaven's light.
So should the Sufi cast away that night.

Because you came here blazing like a star
A lamp of heaven. Now know who you are!

THE BRIGHTER

No candle can withstand the blazing sun
Love is but dissolution in the One

So come dissolve, come completely resign
Leaving no trace as you become the Sign.

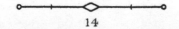

TWO WINES

Let carnal souls drink of the wines of hell
The wine of heaven, an infinite well

Is for the souls with divine intellect
To take them to the place of no regret

The donkey's allegiance is to his gut
His heart's desire is to eat and rut

Issah drank from the fount of the divine
Inviting all who thirst to share the wine

Which is proportion's elixir itself
O traveller, don't leave it on the shelf

But choose that wine the divine vessel holds
Its nasha through all holy texts unfolds

Promising in heaven, heaven's grace
And on earth the reason's measured pace.

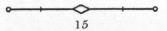

CAUSE AND EFFECT

The branch exists only to bear the fruit
The knowledge of which resides in the root

Would a gardener plant and tend the vine
Without the promise of the grape and wine?

Before this truth let all your reason pause
What you thought was effect, is but the cause.

FORM

How futile form and harmony
If ears don't hear or eyes don't see.

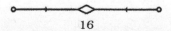

REACH OUT

Reach out for the world
through every sense

Colors, music, sex,
wine and incense

The five ladders on
which a man attains

The heights of pleasure
and sensual planes

The inner senses,
hidden in the heart

Will carry man
to those planes apart

Yet on that journey
expect suffering

And pain that very
ecstasy may bring

To the body while
enriching the soul

And thus enriching,
make the body whole.

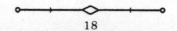

DESTROY TO BUILD

Destroy the house to find the treasure chest
Then, when the treasure's found, you may invest

In building there a palace even more
Sumptuous than the one there was before.

Raze the fort from which the devil gloats
Build it anew with towers, ramparts, moats

His powers won't bend to your earthly wish
Spiritual power was sent to astonish

You and me with the wonder of His ways
From purple dawn to sunset's orange haze.

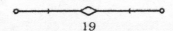

PHARAOH THE RICH

God granted Pharaoh every luxury
And all that could be wished for, so that he

Never felt the pinch of suffering
Or need. He lacked no earthly thing,

Which made him proud and negligent and vain
The attributes of those who don't feel pain.

So Pharaoh never turned his face in prayer
Behaving as though God was never there.

Now God has granted every soul some grief
So that we may call for His relief

And invite the Healer into our pain
To cure the heart and wipe the mark of Cain.

While pharaohs have the cravings of their lust
Satisfied with their empires of dust.

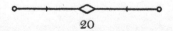

THE FURNACE

My soul's a furnace happy with the fire
That burns within—its nature is desire

For Love. My friend, if you don't wish to burn
In that same fire—you have a lot to learn.

LOVE IS SURRENDER

O youth in love, fall at her feet
Without your beloved, you are incomplete

God's fabric comes from Adam and Eve
As intertwined as threads of the weave.

LOGIC AND DESIRE

Logic will bargain through twists and bends
Desire is careless of where it all ends.

THE BLASPHEMERS

You kept company, O Rumi, with blasphemers who
swore
Their cursing
God's house
meant
they hadn't shut the door.

TODAY

Tomorrow is a hope—the dreamer's way
The Sufi lives the moment, rejoices in today!

PRAYER AND PRIDE

Do not be proud of saying prayers, they can never be
What you, Son of Man, mistake for intimacy

With God. Go, offer words to that empty sky—
Who the hell are you that He should reply?

THE KNOWLEDGE

From father to son it passes, my friend, the belief −
Learn now its value or come elsewhere to grief.

FLEAS

Don't burn the blanket infested with a single flea
Don't turn away from the human who is as flawed as
thee.

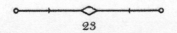

THE DUMB CAN SPEAK

The word of the Book can be spoken by the dumb
Say in your heart, "When the help of God shall come."

MIRRORS

The Prophet said the faithful are mirrors to each other
You in subjugation are no better than your brother

To seek solace in humankind
is the way of fools

Earthly loves,
are shattered mirrors,

Or are but mangled tools.

KINSHIP

To speak the same language is one form of kin
Yet that which unites is the language within

One Turk and the other may share the same tongue
Do they hear the same music when the heart's song
is sung?

TONGUE

Your tongue, O rambling friend,
Can make heaven on earth its double
And yet your tongue, O Rumi,
Is the fount of all your trouble!

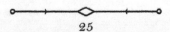

SOLOMON AND SHEBA

Sheba knew that King Solomon was
Fated for her virgin bed because

The marriage between wealth and wisdom would
Conspire to bequeath the world the good

Which both their realms in troubled times desired.
Besides which she was awesomely inspired

By what she heard of his inventive wit
And charm and strength. She knew she wanted it.

She sent him forty mules loaded with bricks
Of gold and a ring wound in a helix

But when this mule train reached Solomon's realm
They saw a plain of gold spread before them.

So on and on they walked for forty days
Shielding their eyes from its reflected rays

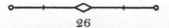

And thinking "Where the hell have we been sent?
This gold is but this kingdom's fundament!

We may as well have brought a pile of dust
To Solomon." The intelligent must

Reconsider their intelligence
Which may be commoner than common sense.

But Solomon was mildly amused
His wise reply was subtly interfused

With sarcasm. "Why do you bring me gifts?
Observe instead the loving hand that shifts

The planets and the stars and moves the sun
O leave your gold, unite me with the One

Who created every moving galaxy
And gave us light so that our eyes might see."

Then Solomon sent Sheba's servants back
To tell their queen of gold he had no lack

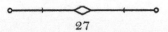

In a land which was constructed of the stuff
And though rejection may seem a bit rough

A little thought would help her understand
That he was merely trying to lend a hand

To lead her from the vanity of thrones
Out of this vale of tears and sighs and groans

To where the wandering Ibrahim did find
The peace of that which resides in the mind

The light that Yusuf found when he emerged
And found the darkness of his hell was purged

By revelation. Though it may sound strange
O Queen, embrace the alchemy of change!

USE WHAT HE HAS GRANTED YOU

Use what He has granted you, my friend
While shafts exist the bow must not unbend

His word is sharp and always hits the spot
Unlike the quibbles "if," "maybe" and "what!"

He is the sunlight slicing through the dark
He is the silence of the twilit park

The body is but that which must endure
And love is what we must be grateful for

Laughter is the caged beast in your breast
Unleash it now before you go to rest

I want to be surrounded by your love
As a hand is covered by a fitting glove

Does love infest your soul and every sense?
The colours of the world are evidence

Of divine waters, divine time and space
Reflected in the lines of Shams's face.

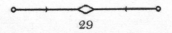

DOUBT

You are the thoughts that sowed my mind with doubt
You are the secret longing to get out.

LIKE THIS

How does the longing turn itself to bliss?
Raise your eyes and smile and say: "Like this!"

The song of love, the story of a kiss
Is easy to recount; it's just like this!

All souls return, O sceptic don't dismiss
The fact that I can return home: like this!

Don't ever stoop to sniff out the spirit
Whose scent is beyond sense and human wit

Just lean forward, let's be cheek to cheek
You will have found the fragrance that you seek.

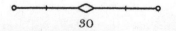

If someone asks how Issah raised the dead
There is no answer. Nothing I have read

Can tell me how it's done, but I know this
The closest explanation, is a kiss

The pain of passion is akin to fire
Loving leaves me with traces of desire

The crack that rents and stills a broken heart
Is that which forces heaven's doors apart.

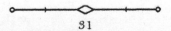

SCIENCE

Trees are rooted in the ground,
They fear
The sound of sawing wood
—It draws near

They are the prey of every
saw-toothed will
Because they draw their life
by standing still

The Tigris and Euphrates
would be,
Without their flow, as salty
as the sea.

And both the sun and moon give
out their light
As sparks in the machine of day
and night

The air that's trapped in caverns
becomes stale
How different from the breeze that
fills a sail!

So movement is the law –
The law that rules the skies
Issah caused the dead to
cast off their shrouds and rise
by breathing into dust a living soul
saying, 'Rise, your faith had made thee whole!'

Signs and symbols
stories I recall,
should lead you on a journey
That is all!

LOVE IS ALL

Love is all there is and that's not new
I've heard that all my life—and so have you

But love is also that which guarantees
That you pass through heaven's doors with ease

So what then is this "love?" My heart be still!
What more is it than melting of the will

Into the will of that which can't be known?
Or snared in mental traps? That bird has flown

Beyond the clouds of knowing. Now submit!
If there's a truth on earth, this is it.

*

Love is that which makes the bitter sweet
Love is that which charms a leaden sheet

Into a solid plate of gold. Love can
Heal a wound and cure the ailing man

Love can be kind or harsh, it can expose
The cruel thorn pretending it's a rose

Love, the acid that can smelt a stone
It is the spell that makes the sun postpone

Its tryst with dawn. It can delay the light
And grant the lovers that much more of night

Through love the healer resurrects the dead
And bids Sofia to walk with her bed

I had to bring the healer Issah in
God's love sent him to forgive all sin

Embrace God's love and come to Him alone
—And make the scaffold of this world
Your throne.

*

Love knows no king, no slave, no thief, no saint
Love grabs the worst and best without restraint

Love bears us up to answer heaven's call
Would you have guessed he summons
one and all?

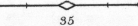

VOICES

All prophets are but windows to the light
You can't say one was wrong and one was right

They are the same, their message is but one
To crave the light, is to accept the sun.

POURING RAIN

Receive his wisdom like the pouring rain
Its source is endless but like harvest grain

It has its season. Though you'll only get
As much as you deserve of it—and yet

He has in store an infinite supply
Available to every passerby

He measures out the wisdom he will dole
In accord with the measure of your bowl.

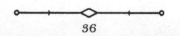

SAMARITANS

To those who cry for help
The Samaritan will come
Drawn to the sound. God knows
There are some

Who seek to help where
It isn't needed.
Their awareness of need
Has superseded

Restraint and caution,
Your desire to please
To diagnose and cure
Means you know the disease.

Or the law that makes
water flow from high to low,
It is absurd to ask,
"How does the water know?

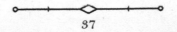

In which direction
It must start?"
Let the music of the spheres
Speak to your heart!

Brush the hair
That falls over your eyes
Unchain your feet
Let them walk the skies

The ecstasy will come
As a mother to a child
If you let your cry break out
—pure, heartfelt and wild!

NASUH

A man named Nasuh, soft of feature
Was often mistaken for a female creature

Satan filled his head with lies
And promises, and suggested he disguise

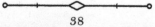

Himself as a woman and find employ
In the Princess's bathhouse. O what joy

He could derive, shampooing the women's hair
And massaging their bodies, what rare

pleasures he would undoubtedly derive
With a permanent hard, what a way to be alive!

So Nasuh did just that. He spent his days
In lustful heaven, to Satan be praise!

Except that soon he heard the voice of his own guilt
Which whispered, "Nasuh you are damned, you built

Your pleasure dome on quicksand, it could sink
If you are caught and executed. Think!"

And foreswear Satan, shun the horned beast
Who leads to famine disguised as a feast.

Hearing this, young Nasuh turned to pray
Acknowledging that he had lost his way.

He sought the advice of a Sufi guide
Who said that men who ran could seldom hide.

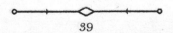

The Sufi said that prayer would intervene
And show him pleasures he had never seen

Nasuh, though chastised, felt like a trapped cur.
Next day the bathhouse was in a mighty stir

The Princess was missing a pair of pearls
The suspects were, of course, the bathhouse girls.

The poor girls were told that they'd be whipped
If they did not submit, so they were stripped.

Nasuh was shampooing a lady's head
And feasting on this naked female spread

And losing concentration Nasuh dropped
The shampoo kettle and his client stopped

Looking in the mirror and turned round
And Nasuh knew that he would now be found

Out and began running towards the door,
When the head eunuch said, "None can leave the floor!

Till I say so and you, take off your robe!"
The game was up, the attendant would probe

His body and delve every orifice
The eunuch asked Nasuh, "Now, what's amiss?"

The only way out now was to confess
That he had several times seen the Princess

Naked as a blossom, from toe to tits
A crime for which he would be chopped to bits.

His heart sank as though it were made of stone
His stomach cramped, he felt very alone

And just as he surrendered to his fate
A eunuch shouted, "Found them! God is great!"

So did he dodge the executioner's sword?
And did he drop and give praise to the Lord?

You bet! He prayed, "I thought my time had come,
Forgive, forgive ..." but Nasuh was struck dumb.

He would forever be downcast, alone
Knowing only he knows, what he has known.

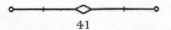

DON'T ASK

My friend
My fellow traveler
Don't ask where I go

The only logical answer
Unhelpful and yet not,
Is that I do not know.

A pen is
An instrument
It doesn't know how to write

Does a ball
Ever know
The trajectory of its flight?

The drunk and
The policeman
Are characters in this play

Pieces on a
Chessboard
Can only move in a certain way.

THE WILL TO DROWN

Desire and your longings will bring you to a fall
Why fear falling, my friend, isn't it after all

Like willing yourself to drown in God and go to
paradise,
To a haven under the waters or a garden in the
skies?

What ecstasy it is to be pierced by the glance
The arrow from a lover's eye, the wound that makes
you dance,

O Heart, what difference then, between joy and pain?
Opposites are identical and logic is in vain.

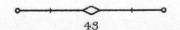

LOSE ALL DESIRE

But for her, your lover wills that you lose all desire
Love, when at its brightest, seeks to quench the fire

Dissolution in that love, they say, resembles death,
Yet it is the paradise where single hearts draw
breath.

HOME

A bird of the rock and sea may come to rest
And take shelter in a tree-bird's nest

And still hear the echoes of shells in her ear
The music by which the seagulls steer

So fly from the nest and leave the tree
Behind. Wing your way to eternity

Leave Adam trapped in his garden home
And Issah blessed to walk on the foam.

BE UNSUBTLE

O thinker addicted to subtle thoughts
Adding infinities and subtracting noughts

Your mind can make angels dance on a pin
O turn to the thoughtless spirit within!

BROTHERS

All brothers should be like grapes on a vine
Pressed together, yielding their wine

The ripe ones hide the green ones taste
Even imperfection doesn't go to waste.

SKEPTIC

O Skeptic who sees nothing in empty space
Think now of infinity as God's face

The images will come if you open your mind
To His word alone and leave doubt behind.

The Baptist's mother came to Mary and said
You shall bear a Son through whom God will raise
the dead

The child and that faith in Mary grew
And Issah was born to heal me and you.

EQUALS

O Muslim, when you stand in the rank of prayer,
You are the fabric of all others, indivisible as the air

The Messenger of God has made you as one
You who were divided, son against son.

THE WORD IS ALL

The Holy Book says, "If the sea were to become ink ..."
And all feathers quill pens, O mortals, do not think,

A syllable could be written to displace the Word
Given to the Messenger and subsequently heard

By writers and poets whose words must, alas, fade
Leaving only His Truth which at your feet is laid.

ON THE JOURNEY

Follow your Guide, Traveler, don't trust to the map
These highways and low ways are prone to mishap

We all travel down the ways we haven't been before
So trust to Him and follow—he'll take you, door to
door.

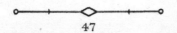

BE PATIENT

The child wants the breast at once, it hasn't learned
to wait
Patience is the key to joy, O Traveler, hesitate!

OPPOSITES

In seeing darkness, O Rumi, you know the light;
You know happiness by feeling sorrow's bite

All meaning hides, till its opposite is known
Save God, with no opposite, He is hidden, alone.

WEAR THE CROWN LIGHTLY

To wear a crown lightly is to be a king
Regardless and regarded as the real thing

Consuming yourself in "Me, me, me!"
The sentence that condemns you to never be.

DEATH IS THE THIEF

Death is the thief who is sure to come
Careless of whom he takes, or takes from

So cling, O Passerby, to what you love the best
Let death and the thief deprive you of the rest.

HE KNOWS

"I know not what he knows, but I know he knows"
Thus the pupil fulfilled from the Master goes.

DEATH BE NOT PROUD

O Rich One, will your silks be your shroud?
Or will you wear the earth and leave death to be
proud?

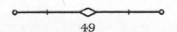

IN THE BEYOND

In the beyond, my friend, there is traffic and trade
In the deeds you stored and the mess you made

What He will count are the treasures of that store
Not your pretence and piety. These are toys, no more

As children set up shop and wed in fantasy
So the world's conceits are but games—let them be!

And when nightfall comes, the child's game ends
He returns home hungry, without his friends.

MATERIAL THE EARTH

Material is the earth and material the stars
O Rumi, seek the spirit—the water not the vase!

ASS

Unruly ass, your kick will only fracture your hoof,
Your stubbornness takes you beyond reason or proof

You live by the laws that you yourself have made
O Adam, your disobedience is heaven's law betrayed!

QUARANTINE

There is no cure for the sickness of the heart
Quarantine all lovers, keep them apart

Affliction though it seems to be, love is God's gift
Anchoring to beauty, the human soul adrift.

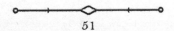

EARTHLY KNOWLEDGE

You acquire earthly knowledge, passerby.
My friend that isn't knowledge, it's a lie!

The only truth you need to know is Him
Only he can fill your measure to its brim.

Knowledge like water flows from high to low
Be humble then, my brother, and let His presence
flow.

FINAL ECSTASY

Reason cannot ever grasp
That final ecstasy
To bring a thinker to his God
Is to make a blind man see

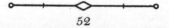

THE MOTE

Observant of your neighbor's sin
You fail to see the fires of hell within

Mullah, Censor, Judge and Hypocrite
You will burn in the fire your arrogance has lit.

LOVE, THE MOTHER AND CHILD

To proclaim His peace, God sent a dove
This messenger of mystery is called Love—Love
herself, though mother of all men,

Is the child of faith and only when

Our faith in Him is strong, she will be seen
As moons emerge from out of their cloudy screen.

And when your faith in Love is waning low
She'll wait behind her veil for faith to grow.

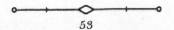

FLY

The fellow feeling of the human race
Is the portrait of His divine face

Your fellow traveller can feel your pain
He shares with you the sin and mark of Cain

If you can free yourself from jealousy
You and the world would venture free

And like the dove the trapper did untie
You can rise up and soar into the sky.

SECRET LOVE

You are the joy that dances in my breast
My secret love that's hidden from the rest

The miser's coin will sometimes leave the purse,
So you escape and give birth to my verse.

UNSCHOOLED PROPHET

Galen's potions could not conquer death
As Issah could with just one healing breath.

Moses with his single wooden staff
Conquered Pharaoh who was king of half

The known world. All philosophical claim
Was by an unschooled prophet put to shame!

THIEVING EYES

O thieving eyes, you're punished for the theft
Of her beauty—now she's turned and left!

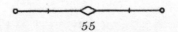

DO NOT GO

I hear you intend to leave me, I hear
You have a new friend, that you call him, "dear"

How could you wound your constant lover so
And threaten this estrangement? Please don't go,

O moon for whom the very heavens shake
What betrayal is this? How can you take

The promise we exchanged so lightly now
And fob me off with some insincere vow?

O you who command paradise and hell
You whose eyes weave heaven's dizzy spell

How could you mix this poison in the sweet
How could a lover turn to such deceit?

My soul's an open furnace for your flame
Yet you leave it darkened, O the shame

Of being abandoned. Lover, do not go
Leave the moon of my night still aglow

Your leaving is the drought, my lips are dry
The only moisture, wells up in my eye.

HE LIVES

They told me the immortal one had died
I threw their words back in their teeth—they lied!

Who dares to say the sun has left the skies?
Who would embrace the eclipse of his eyes?

IN DISGRACE

Beside myself I wander in disgrace
To catch a glimpse of my beloved's face

I circle the bazaars and roam the streets
Through drunken dens and muttering retreats

Admitting I am drunk and full of sin
I knock at your locked door,
O, let me in!

Thousands take the plunge of ecstasy
Deliver but one pearl of truth to me

Jalal of Rome through ecstasy does rave
Protesting he is Shams the Master's slave.

BE STILL

Be still as stone
Refrain from speech
And laughter

You shall be given
A silken tongue
In the world, hereafter.

EXPERIMENT

Try this experiment
and think of nought
But only that
which creates all thought.

THE PRISON

When God has made the earth for you to roam
Why have you made a prison cell your home?

TRUE MOSQUE

Do not praise and magnify the mosque
However beautiful, it is the husk

And not the grain. Go seek the holy saints,
By delving in their hearts, the soul acquaints

Itself with where the fount of life resides
And where the light of Him alone abides.

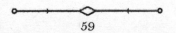

ATTRIBUTES

One attribute of God is that he sees
Every atom's movement and of these

Our lives are made and all the worlds revolve.
We call him "knowing" because he can solve

What are to us dilemmas but to him
Are a millionth part of his creative whim.

These are no simple names that men invent
They have not come about by accident

But are the qualities of that first cause
That gave us life and disciplines and laws.

THE FRIEND

Go my friends and fetch the Friend to me
He stays away, he lingers wantonly

He'll try and say he'll come another day
Just ignore that and fetch him anyway.

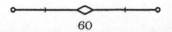

MESSAGE TO A STAR

Last night I gave a message to a star
To carry to the moon, however far

To deliver to the sun whose rays can turn
The rocks to golden emblems as they burn.

I bared my breast and pointed to the pain
Just so the star could make my message plain

You rock the crib to give an infant rest
My pounding heart I cradled in my breast

And yet my heart for hunger was not still
It wouldn't find its fulfilment until

He who all the multitude doth feed
Would lend his love to my heart's fervent need.

He is the heartache all I say to him
Is, "Saki, fill my cup up to the brim."

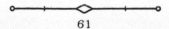

ELEMENTS

Man was not made of water
nor of fire,
wind or clay.

The spirit of desire
Has made us what we are
and we transcend.

So don't dabble
In this babble
Of elements, my friend.

LIGHT ON LIGHT

A hundred beings like me can turn to dust
A thousand take my place who in Him trust

"Why," he asks, "do you gaze in my face?"
"You are the light that dominates all space."

So where else in creation would I look?
You are the stars, the ocean, mountain, brook.

As Ishmael turned his bare breast to the knife
To Abraham and Him I give my life

Of flamboyance my love is now accused
My heart's a drum, its beating is excused

By he who sent an Issah to the fight
To spread the vision of the light on light.

ROSES

Lovers find the roses,
A tangle of thorns poses

No threat to lovers' hands
Love's innate reason stands

Logic on its head
And postulates instead

The way of the sixth sense—
The lovers' intense

Vision can expose
Arenas beyond those

In which logic operates.
As the Sufi vacates

The earthbound Mullah's chair
He knows he would go where

His heart would find its use
He would embrace the noose

Knowing that even death
Breathes in every breath

So friend, deny the thorn—
Be to the rose reborn.

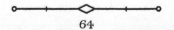

MAJNUN

Majnun loved Layla with total passion
Though demonstrative love wasn't the fashion

He seemed indifferent to the supreme hurt
To him dust was gold and gold was dirt.

To Majnun the material world was nought
She was entwined in every living thought.

Love granted him supreme protection—
His body gave off a sweet confection

Which could keep wild beasts at bay.
So Majnun took the lover's way

Which is the way of all desire:
Come melt with Majnun, in the fire

Only vision can transcend
And grant the vision of the end

Who is the one beyond all worth?
Who boils the seas and shakes the earth?

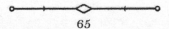

CAPACITY

Moonlight stretches out against the skies
Your share of it depends upon the size

Of windows in your room. Your glass of wine
Dictates the granted measure of divine

Infinite love; and you'll receive His grace
According to the breadth of your embrace.

MOSES AND THE SHEPHERD
(For Moin Khan)

Moses once passed a shepherd at his prayer
And paused to hear this simple man declare

His love for God by promising to tend
To the Almighty's every need and lend

Him all the comforts that he could afford
Promising milk and honey to the Lord.

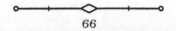

Hearing which Moses flew into a rage
He asked the shepherd, "How can you engage

In idle bribes and chatter in this way
With Him Infinite, and how dare you pray

To God as though he were some needy friend?
Stop offering these silly things and bend

Your body and your mind in total awe
And pray as you were taught to pray. No more

Of babbling about baubles to the King
Of all the heavens that infinite thing

Which surpasses all our worlds and resides
Beyond the light of a thousand suns, besides

You must know that we mortals have no right
To involve God in our miserable plight."

So saying, Moses left the shepherd and
Went on to prophesy to all the land.

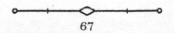

Then God breathed these words into Moses's ear
"You know that shepherd? You were too severe

With the poor man; he wanted to convey
His love for me, so he began to pray

And what he said came straight from his heart
You must have heard, he was willing to part

With anything he owned or thought would please
What better worshippers are there than these?

To tell the truth, Moses, prayer has no form
Like inner lightning, shapeless as a storm

In its sincerity resides its force
No other value shapes this intercourse.'

Then Moses sought the shepherd out again
To admit that he was in error when

He interrupted him and specified
How he should pray. Then on that same hillside

Both Moses and that joyful Shepherd knelt
And each offered a prayer that was heartfelt.

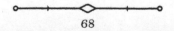

THE POWER OF LOVE

The power of love is to contradict
Its raging and its roaring can be tricked

Into the softness of a fading star
Love does not care a whit for who you are

He says, "Don't come and clutter up my space."
He passes through our lives and leaves no trace

He says, "You are the candle"—it's a joke,
He knows I am a humble spume of smoke

Love says, "You are my guru and my guide"
Mocking the one who never can decide

Which way to go and how and where and why
And whether birds with wings were meant to fly.

And then a subtle change did overcome
The rippling shadows separated from

The fountain of all light which is the sun
And suddenly the light and shade are one.

The chess master in silence moves his piece
I'm grateful for the game—for this release!

AYAZ AND THE PEARL

The king held a pearl
It covered half his hand
He asked a courtier what it was worth
"More gold than we have in all the land."

"Then take the pearl and crush it,"
Demanded the king
"How can I waste the kingdom's wealth
By doing such a thing?"

The minister said and handed
Back the precious gem
The king rewarded him with gold
And the title of knight of the realm

Choosing one by one the king
Questioned all his lords
And receiving the same answer
Handed out rewards

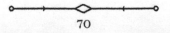

Until he came to Ayaz
And asked him what he thought
The price was. Ayaz said,
"No price. It can't be bought."

The king then handed him the pearl
And went through his charade
Ayaz took a couple of stones
And crushed the pearl so hard

That it crumbled into powder
It was reduced to dust
The king asked Ayaz, "Why?"
He said, "A humble servant must

Obey the king's every wish
And honor the king's word
Above the price of a shiny stone."
When the other princes heard

Ayaz, they regretted
Their worldly conceit
And flung themselves
At their monarch's feet.

And begged him for his mercy
He ordered his axe to chop
Off their heads but Ayaz
Arose and bade him stop.

"Let them live, O King
And allow them to hope
For union with you. Spare
The knife and axe and rope

They should not be punished
These are but herded sheep
Or say they fell to error
Following others like sleep-

Walkers or like drunkards
Going where others lead
I was drunk with obedience
So let me intercede

For my friends and co-sinners
And punish them only when
I am sober, because I
Shall never be sober again.

Those who bow are changed
And whomsoever prostrates
Himself before the king
By that act alone creates

A new man. Every gnat
That falls into your drink
Will absorb its essence
And in the wine will sink

As I, O King, have sunk
Or been crushed like this pearl
So let this manic mystery
Endlessly unfurl."

THE LIGHT INSIDE

The light you radiate you cannot trace
Back to the womb. Your features and your face

Did not begin in semen. Do not hide
In veils of anger all the light inside.

THE FIERCEST BEAST

Leave the nightingale, who is pure sound,
Ignore the peacock stamping on the ground

In ecstasy. His colours will waylay
Your mind. Become the tiger stalking prey

Or like the sun, the eagle from the East,
Imitate the planet's fiercest beast.

BLUSHES

Silent blushes came to my cheek
Till you taught me to sing,
Taught me to speak.

In shyness I would decline
The offer of life's liquor
Now you ply me with wine

In forbidding solemnity I would pray
Now children make faces
And mock me in their play.

THE COURT

There is the age-old custom among kings
That like the eagle, he should spread his wings

With every feather on his left, a knight,
And scribes and scholars, the feathers on the right.

The Sufi masters have to stand before
Him—mirrors of their souls, the open door

Which lets in light to show kings who they are
O king and courtiers, gaze upon that star!

POWER OF A PRAYER

Do not misuse the power of a prayer
Out of bitter envy, defeat or despair
God will not answer destructive whims
He'll either ignore it or punish you—beware!

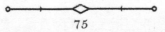

SUFI'S WISDOM

To seek a sufi's wisdom do not go
To books or ink or pages, rather know
That all his wisdom can be found within
A human heart that is as white as snow.

WOMAN

A woman is of God's radiance a ray
Not just a thing with which man has his way
When God created Eve, she was to be
The source of all creative interplay.

LIFE

We came from Him, the one who is unseen
From out the garden which is evergreen
And hence to him my friend we must return
This life is but a moment in between.

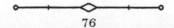

TONGUE

O tongue, you are the fount of countless gems
The artisan of complex diadems
You are also the spring of all disease
The plague that withers roses on their stems.

LIGHT ON RUBBISH

Behold the light that falls on rubbish heaps
Illuminating filth, and yet it keeps
Its purity. So heaven's radiance shines
On humanity, which below it creeps.

WISEST SCHOLAR

O wisest Mullah that has ever been
With the longest beard the world has seen
Look in the mirror of the world and time
Behold the timeless barber shaves you clean!

FIND THE ONE

If the touchstone of your heart and head
Can differentiate the gold from lead,
Then lead the way and spread the light
But if it can't—find one who can instead!

THE FISH-HOOKED LINE

The actions of your body should define
If to the good or bad you do incline
The body is a reel that must obey
The mind that pulls it like a fish-hooked line.

DAVID'S MUSIC

The melodies of David's lyre could
Melt the hearts of those who understood
But to the faithless and the faithless ear
They were but twanging of strings on wood.

ENMITY OF THE WISE

The Sufi says the enmity of wise
Men is preferable to the honeyed lies
Of the fool, who professes all his love
And pleads his earnestness with vacant sighs.

THE ASS

The ass will through his stubbornness
Run into the wild
His master seeks to bring him back
Like a prodigal child

Not simply because he can get
More labour from the beast
But to prevent him in the wild,
Becoming a tiger's feast.

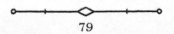

CONTRARY

There are those so contrary
They sicken from the cure
So save your stories, Rumi,
For seekers of the pure.

THE BEYOND

Sufi, seek not to understand
The mind or will of he who planned
This universe before which our
Whole world is but a speck of sand.

THE HEART SINGS

So bear my body to the grave, my friends,
But hear my heart whose singing never ends

No time now for your wailing or your tears
My death is not at all what it appears.

The grave is not the sum of life complete
It is the veil of lovers, their retreat

Beyond the compass of logic and mind
Leaving the chain of separateness behind.

You saw the dust settling, now see it rise
Think of me with Him and shut your eyes

Locked beneath the earth my soul is free
To be with Him for all eternity.

SEED

A seed in fertile soil can always grow
A human caught in the eternal flow

Of water, springing from the only source
Believes that life and death will take their course

But this is an illusory belief
The mind has stolen truth, it is a thief

A sinking sun is rising elsewhere too
My grave is but the last door to the new

World which is His abode, it is the place
Beyond the flood where we are face to face.

THE EVIL PLANTER

He who spreads evil
Is one who plants weeds

Don't waste your words
Don't sell him rose seeds.

BEAUTY

Whatever comes to beauty
Is beauty's reward
For a good woman, the good man
For the empty scabbard, a sword.

Children of the light are born
To help us see the way
And they attract each other
Emanating the ray

Of that eternal fire.
The passion of the world
Will only leave some ashes
Weightless, crumbling, curled.

SURROUNDINGS

Beyond Eden's gate
The horrors lie in wait

Surrounding hell's fire
Are the things we desire.

THE LOAD

My friend, assist your neighbour with his load
Easing his burden puts you on the road

To heaven's rest. Biting the bitter skin
Of sugarcane lets out the sweet within.

This world will put you to the test of pain
This is the way of all spiritual gain.

DISGUISE

A veil of madness can disguise a saint
What seems real could be canvas and paint

True sight is not in the eyes but in the heart
Beware of deceptions of both man and art.

MOSES IN THE REEDS

The Mother of Moses fervently feeds
The child she will abandon to the reeds

She puts a future prophet to the test
And tears the crying infant from her breast

She bends over and lets the cradle go
This infant will eventually know

Who he is, the secret of his birth
As we recall the heavens from this earth.

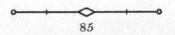

ENVY

Envy is a poison
An illogical distress

The fact your neighbor has more
Doesn't mean that you have less.

GRAVITY

God is like gravity
All things fall
Towards him. Homing
To the stall
The scattered pigeons
Will return.
He who can
In a rock discern
The face or form
That it conceals,

He has the skill
Of the sculptor
He reveals
A shape and can hone
The figure from the stone
He has
The gift, of God alone.

ALEPPO

"Does this road lead to Aleppo?"
Your answer can be "yes" or "no"
Your opinion doesn't make it so
Consult a map before you go!

THE COMPASSIONATE EYE

Many a tear falls
From the compassionate eye
The time has now come for it
To see itself and cry.

CLEANSED

The bough is cleansed as the storm sweeps,
The candle brightens as its wax weeps.

ONENESS

Don't try to separate
The stem from the root,
Is not the flautist's breath
But a part of the flute?

HE LISTENS

There are no rules of worship
He will hear
The voice of every heart
That is sincere.

CHILD'S PLAY

Say, "Goo-goo" and "glug-glug"
Or sing a lullaby
To hell with your high intellect
The baby mustn't cry

So does the Sufi
With no stain of condescension
Bring the essence of Him
To our frail attention.

WILD DOG

Stop the wild dog's bite with a muzzle
Love is the solution to that eternal puzzle

What is your destiny? What is your duty?
Give way to love, give way to beauty

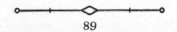

The trapper seeks the waterfowl in every stream
The form of your beloved, haunts your every dream

If you turn off your reason, switch off the light
Will she step out of your dream?
She might, she might!

TO EACH IS GIVEN

God never gave
His bigger beasts a sting
He gave it to the bee
With an invisible wing

And with the skill of storing
Sweetness in the hive.
The silkworm spins its gossamer
In order to survive

However large, the elephant
Has no such subtle skill
God gives to each his powers
His wonders to fulfill.

NAMES

God taught the earthly Adam
To name all things although
He taught the angels only
What he wanted them to know

PEARLS

You aren't a single jewel
You're an ocean of pearls

You can be a planet
Which in its orbit whirls

Around the sun. Or you shall be
An angel and sprout wings

And then come face to face
With the maker of all things.

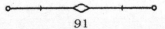

THROUGH A GLASS

He who looks at wine
Through colored glass
Knows not the color of the wine.
Reflected light must pass

Through the filter of the cup
And yet the wine
Remains what it is.
God's design

Cannot be filtered
Through the mind
Or through your reason strained,
Through patience and
Surrender only
Can it be attained.

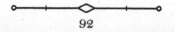

PAINTERS

Greeks from the West and Chinese from the East
Were invited to the Sultan's great feast

The Sultan being a man of many parts
Was interested in Sport and in the Arts

The rival painters from the East and West
Began to argue about who could best

Do justice to the senses. Who could paint
The truthful artefact that would acquaint

The beholder with Wonder. Painting should
Seduce and teach if it were any good.

"So leave behind your rivalry and start,"
The Sultan said, "to demonstrate your Art."

He assigned to each group a studio
And challenged each of them in time to show

The skills they boasted. The Chinese asked the king
For a thousand colors. The Greeks asked nothing

But stuff they said they'd use to clean the rust.
Then from their studio out came clouds of dust

Each day. The studios were contiguous and
Were separated by a heavy, bland

Gray curtain. The Sultan did then assign
To both the delegations a deadline.

And finally arrived the judgment day:
The king ordered in turn they should display

What they had done, and so first the Chinese
Unveiled their work; exquisite expertise

Was portrayed on the walls for all to see
The Sultan was impressed and publicly

Rewarded these artists who could portray
The earth, the sky and even winds at play

The painting was an obvious delight
That silenced speech and mesmerized the sight

Of all who gazed upon it. Now the team
Of Greeks were called even though it did seem

That nothing could outclass that Chinese art
The king ordered the curtain drawn apart

And it was done. There was no paint upon
The walls but they were polished and they shone

Like mirrors made of silver, shiny, pale
Reflecting the painting in each detail

Perfectly. The Sultan could see this art
Was like an installation of the heart

Because the pure heart in reflection can
Display the works of God and not of man.

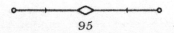

IN HIS WORKS

In his myriad works
Does the maker exist
If you had no fingers
You couldn't form a fist.

THE MAN WHO CRIED

The man who cried, "O Allah"
Each day in his prayer
Was persuaded by Evil
That God wasn't really there.

The proof was that every day
He prayed to the Supreme One
And each day didn't he notice,
That answer came there none?

Hearing this the pious man
Fell into deep despair
And complained to Ezekiel,
"God doesn't hear my prayer."

Then Ezekiel said, "Pious one
It's not that he hasn't heard
When you call him 'Allah'
His answer is in that word."

ROMANCE

It was stories that first gave me
The idea of romance
I kept my young eyes open
Waiting for the trance

That would fall on me, strike me,
Heavenly Cupid's dart
Till I realized that you
Were already in my heart.

THE DIFFERENCE

Together as one with you I lie awake
Alone, I suffer this relentless ache

Ecstasy and pain, all lovers have seen them
Bless Him that we know the difference between them

THE CAP

A man gave me a cap
You the brain that reasons under it

A man made me a robe
And you the form on which it proudly rests

A man gave me gold
And you, the sense and hand that counts it

A man gave me a horse
And you, the reins and skill to guide it

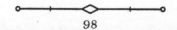

A man held up a lamp
Where did I get the eyes to see its light?

A man may bring me sweets
Where comes the devouring hunger and the taste?

Men can give me subsistence
But He alone gives me the life that needs it

Men gift me treasure
You bring true blessings

Men build a house
You, the earth on which it stands

And Yours is the house
In which all are nourished

You were the one who created the gold
You the provider of gifts untold

Yours was the hand that made men generous
Teaching them the gift of giving

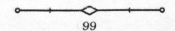

Yours is the hand that kneaded clay
And turned it into the world of the living

And then from nothing
The eternal sky

And spread the
Carpet of the earth

You fashioned the
Torches of the stars

And in your image
Gave us birth

So man is a shimmer
Of exaltation

Reasons and Spirit
Are his signs

As over and in
The passing water

The moon reflected
Nightly shines.

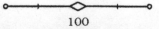

WHEN IT IS REVEALED

When that which is now hidden is revealed
To you and beauty draws aside her veil

The phial of perfume is finally unsealed
And you may sip from out the holy grail

These assembled elements of delight
Will launch a new star in the starlit night.

KINGS AND SLAVES
(A Tribute to Arabi)

All kings are only servants to their slaves
Humans ready to die for Him who saves

Them from death. Traps are there to serve the bird
And sons of Adam, captives of the Word

So lose your hearts to the idea of loss
The lowest number always wins the toss.

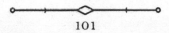

BEHIND THE VEIL

My beloved is hidden by that veil
Try and conjure her face and you will fail
What your eyes cannot conjure my heart sees
Her perfume is the scent upon the breeze.

THE TRANCE

I fell into a trance
And was in my beloved's garden
I was drunk through dance
And incoherently begged her pardon

The flowers of existence
Had burst in peacock bloom
But then I woke up sober
Locked within a room.

The garden's gone and there's
A pain inside my head
And though I'm separated from
The dream, it isn't dead.

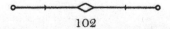

102

LAND OF LOVE

This fairyland of love
Is a country to cry for
Getting lost in you
Is a loss to die for

I said, "I will make love to you
Then fade upon the air."
She was appalled and said,
"Don't you even dare!"

CATASTROPHES

Catastrophes, contrivances
The latest heinous crime
Are passing shows, the real news
Is the stillness beyond time.

AT THE PARTY

The party was crowded—
Of our secret love
I could give you no token.
They started a game of whispers,
I put my cheek to yours,
My heart was broken.

SOUNDS

The winds of the deserts
Set up a wail
To match the songs
Of the nightingale

Each sound was the message
She sent today
Echoing over rooftops
And far away.

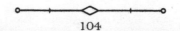

THE PEARL

Death holds no terror for the one who can
See beyond this life's short and fitful span

The knock of rocks, the churning ocean's swell
Do not affect the pearl inside the shell.

ISSAH AND THE FOOLS

Issah the healer
(To him all praise)
Had the Word from God
Which was able to raise

The dead and breathe
Life into a wraith
Not to crowd the planet
But to bring us to faith

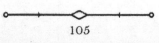

In the living God. But he
Walked with men who were
Self-seeking in their depth
And deeply insincere

They pressed him for the formula
They begged him for the word
The mantra that would raise the dead
And by Him be heard

So Issah in his innocence
Whispered it to those
Jackals who were present
When Lazarus arose

And gave to all of us,
The doubting human race,
Faith in the eternal
Life, faith in Allah's grace.

These jackals, jubilating, went
Through a desert full of stones
And came across a scattered pile
Of whitened, sun-bleached bones.

When one of these self-seekers
More foolish than the rest
Thought he'd put the formula
And Issah to the test.

He uttered the dreaded word of life
While facing to the East
And from the bones there came alive
A predatory beast,

Who ate the entire company
The miracle-maker too
Now Rumi that's the story
But the moral must come through.

Issah was no magician
His miracles weren't magic
The fools who deny Allah
Their ends will be farcical, tragic.

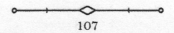

THE WANDERER

It isn't aimlessly through streets
And bazaars that I wander
It's for a glimpse of her, my love
Intoxicated, I squander

My time like a vagabond
Weaving idle rings
Around my lover's haunts
And yet consciousness clings

To that one purpose. I beg
You, have mercy on me Lord
A sinful wretch distraught,
How can broken hearts afford

To be still? A million souls
Delved in this ocean's swell
Searching in their hearts
For the pearl inside the shell

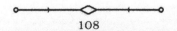

So come, my love, be kind to him
They call the Maulana of Rome
Who is but the slave of Shams-e Tabrizi
A wanderer without a home.

BUTTERFLY WINGS

The air is hardly moved
By butterfly wings that flutter.
O mortal, leave your prayers and seek
The one whose name you utter!

ONLY IN THE DEAD OF NIGHT

Only in the dead of night
Will she lift the veil
The laws of light and modesty
Inevitably prevail

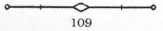

In the harsher light of day.
Did not the burning bush
Appear to Moses in the night?
Lover, do not push

Me into daylight's brutal glare,
It's only in the night
That lovers who by day are blind
Attain their radiant sight.

POUR OUT THE WINE

Pour out the wine that He alone dispenses
Enrich my soul by soaking all my senses

Give it defiance, teach my soul to fly
Pour one more cup, O Saki, one more sigh

May coax the wine out from the heart of stone
Leave him that way who lives by bread—alone.

For bread is that which makes the body whole
But leaves unnourished the flowering soul

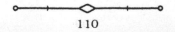

Open for me, Saki, the flask divine
Pour me a measure of celestial wine

And shut the eye that only evil sees
And open that which apprehends the breeze

Let temples and mosques crumble into dust
I am content to drown in divine lust.

EVIDENCE

Once in Hindustan some sages took
An elephant into a pitch-dark room
They wanted scientifically to look
At the ways in which human beings assume

That they discern the spirit from the clues
Their senses can pick up and misdirect
Their judgement, which is how we all abuse
Our senses and God-given intellect.

The first man came and with an outstretched hand
Touched the elephant on his trunk and cried,
"I've got it now, I clearly understand,
This beast is like a pipe that's one foot wide."

Then the sages brought in the second man
Who gestured blindly till he felt an ear
"I know!" he said. "This beast is like a fan
Floppy and stiff, I think that much is clear."

The third fellow to enter touched the leg
Of the elephant though he could not see
He leaned back saying, "No, no, no, I beg
To differ from my friends, obviously

The beast is nothing but a pole."
The fourth man came and grabbed the beast's tail
And said, "At last an idea of the whole
Beast has formed, my instincts never fail."

He declared the elephant was a rope.
So my friends do not count the evidence
Of hand or eye or ear and ever hope
That these can lead beyond the realm of sense.

THE KING AND THE SLAVE GIRL

There was a king in olden times
Who ruled this world and half the next
An amorous individual,
Today we'd call him oversexed.

This king went hunting with his men
And on the road he saw a slave
Girl who took his fancy so
He raised a hand and by this gave

The order to forego the hunt.
He commanded the girl be brought
To him. The price her owners asked
They should be paid. Thus she was bought.

The king with no care for the girl
Indulged his lust and had his way
But that poor child began to fade
And became haggard day by day.

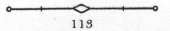

The king felt like the man who bought
An ass and saddle at the fair
And lost the ass to wild beasts,
Was left with the saddle, riding air.

The king called all his doctors to
Attend to the girl and find a cure.
But despite all their efforts she
Withered as the moon before

The darkening nights till she became
As thin as the breadth of a hair.
The proud physicians had not called
On God. The king was in despair

And went barefoot and humble to
The mosque. He touched the floor in prayer
And soaked the mat in royal tears
He prayed and begged that God would spare

The girl he had possessed in lust.
The king collapsed into a faint
And in that fit a vision came
A man would arrive and acquaint

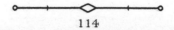

The king and his court physicians
With the secret of the cure
And sure enough when he awoke
The first person whom he saw

Was that promised man of dreams
Sent to him in token of
God's answer to his heartfelt plea
God's return for his professed love.

The king took him into the harem
Took him to where the sick girl lay
The physician examined her
And said, "These medicines that they,

Your court physicians, ministered,
And all the cures that they have tried
Have made the girl's condition worse
The poor patient might have died.

They gave her draughts to heal her flesh
Using all their craft and art
This sickening is not of the flesh
She's dying of a broken heart."

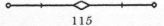

The illness of the heart is ever
Far worse than the body's pain
To cure its painful consequence
The patient must be born again

Into the love beyond preferring.
This love transcendent has no name
It renders all definition
Inadequate, sterile, lame.

All the pens that pen the verses
Poets singing songs of praise
To this mysterious emotion
Are like men who try to gaze

Straight into the sun at noon
Blinding their eyes to see its face,
Instead, they should study shadows
And so comfortably trace

Where the sun is and how bright,
Be satisfied with oblique clues
We know the spirit by the body
Suns and shadows interfuse

Our world. Then that dream physician
Asked the king if he might see
The slave girl and extract her story,
Interview her privately.

The king agreeing, the good doctor
Asked the girl where she was born
And other questions, like a needle
Probing for the painful thorn

That was causing her distraction
The arrow that had torn apart
The breast of this benighted maiden
Piercing her bleeding heart.

He asked her about all her trials
And the masters she had had
She gave him the honest answers,
Her life though so short, was sad

The doctor probed her to find
At what point her pulse would race
And when he named a far-off city
She was like a deer in chase

Frightened by the sound of pursuit
Or like a slave at the command
Of a strict and cruel master
The name he'd used was "Samarkand."

Now he knew the thing that ailed her
That destroyed her heart and soul
He asked her where he lived. She answered,
"Ghatafar in Sar-e Pol."

She told the doctor his professions;
Goldsmith, jeweler, artisan
The doctor determined that he
Would get the king, to find this man

And bring him thence from Samarkand
So that the king could execute
His rival in love. Now he said,
"This heartache that has grown acute

Will now become a wish fulfilled.
Promise me you'll never say
The name Samarkand out aloud."
And saying thus he went his way.

The doctor conferred with the king
Agreed a stratagem and planned
To send a delegation to fetch
That goldsmith from Samarkand

The king sent out his invitation
Luring him with gifts of gold
Feeling in his heart that men were
Cattle to be bought and sold.

With the embassy that set out
He sent the best his land could boast
The goldsmith accepting the gifts was
Impatient to meet his host.

Induced away from Samarkand
Innocent and unsuspecting
His party finally arrived
And demanded to see the king.

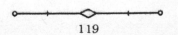

The goldsmith made his salutation
  To the king. The doctor gave
Instructions to the court attendants
To go and fetch the young girl slave

Which they did and as was plotted
The doctor said the king should give
  That poor girl to her lover
  And thus united, let them live

Together and the healing process
  Would contrive to resurrect
Her body back to all its beauty.
  Neither lover did suspect

The king or doctor's bona fides
The embers of their love flared up
Into the flame they had experienced.
  The doctor fed a poisoned cup

To the goldsmith who, in her arms,
  Withered like a sunburnt grape
And shrunk and shriveled by the poison
  The victim lost his human shape.

As he turned ugly, pale and grim
He wasn't what he was before
She couldn't love this withered thing
His ugliness said, "Nevermore."

He wished now he had gone his own way,
And never played love's foolish game
His love had been a self-deception
Born in lust and burnt in shame.

The blood came to his eyes, red rivers
Flowing down his sallow cheeks
"I am the fox killed for his fur
I am that deer the hunter seeks

For meat and musk. The wall does cast
A lengthy shadow as the night
Approaches, but it shortens as
The sun at noon is at its height."

Is what he said before he died
And was erased from memory
The slave girl from her pain and pride
Found release and was set free.

The puzzle is that Rumi says
That though mankind may find it odd
For the murder of this man
The inspiration came from God.

For each one kills the thing he loves
Mortals will not understand
Prepare themselves for sacrifice
Or trust their lives into His hand.

ROOT OF PRIDE

Intelligence can be the root of pride
Your subtle thoughts can take you for a ride

Become a fool, as foolishness is pure
But not the kind of fool who's immature

And makes his dignity a puerile jest.
Negate your intelligence and invest

All faith and reason in the loving Friend
Who is reason's beginning and its end

Submit yourself to Him, the Friend's caress
Can lead the damned out of their wilderness

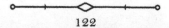

TRUTH AND LIES

The false draws its sustenance from the true
The counterfeit coin's deemed of no value

Only when you can weigh it in a scale
Against some real gold. Truth will prevail

By comparison, which is logic's rule.
He who embraces falsehood is a fool.

THE IRON AND THE FLAME

Iron draws to itself the fiery breath
Of dragons which to humans would mean death.

We living things can only bear the glow
Of gentle suns. Our endurance is so

Much the creation of frailty. But then
The exception to this rule among men

Is the dervish who like iron glows
Red in flame under the hammer's blows.

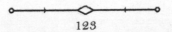

LOVE DIVINE

Afflicted hearts can seek only one cure
The retreat into love will serve as your

Introduction to Him who is the Friend
Before whom souls in supplication bend

And look beyond the endless space of sky
Beyond all time, beyond all "you" and "I"

The vessel of your body can consign
Your soul to the fires of love divine

From which fires all wisdom can disperse
Essences beyond all insights of verse.

I AM YOU

I am the dust that dances in the light
I am the sun that chases out the night

I bid the particles of dust to stay
I beg the sun, "Continue on your way!"

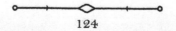

I am that veil of earth, the morning mist
I am the twilight flock of birds that twist

And turn and wheel and return to the nest.
The surf that gives the rocky cliff no rest

And turns again to waves to lash the hull
Of shipwrecked vessels. And I am the skull

Of the body washed up on the coral reef
Time makes no difference between priest and thief

I am the parrot captive in the cage
The silence, word, the whisper, and the rage

Or melody that pours out of the flute
The spark of flint, the candle flame and soot

I am the moth destined for suicide
I am the rose and its fragrance astride

The garden breeze. I am the galaxy
The logic of the evolutionary

Drift. So Jalal ad-Din identify
Yourself as One who says that You are I.

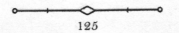

THE SONG OF THE REED

This is the story of the reed that weeps
Tears of separation as it keeps

The memory of parting in lament
And cries for all the pain it underwent

Torn from its bed, O how its heart does yearn
And generates the dream of its return

The knowledge of love and of its caress
The shattered heart knows well and can express

Them better than the heart that's never known
The pain of being in darkness, all alone.

Into the gatherings of men I went
None in those crowds could guess at the extent

Of suffering so hidden in my breast
Because I mingled, disguised like the rest.

No sign of inner turmoil did I send
To each who thought he was my bosom friend.

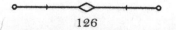

For though we see each other's bodies whole
There is no sight that looks into the soul

The lament of the reed is breathed in fire
If you are cold and deaf to it—retire!

The flame of love comes burning through the flute
Those who cannot hear its song are mute

And cannot of intoxication sing
Though the bird of love be on the wing

I ask you friend, tell me, whoever saw
A thing that was the poison and the cure?

The reed sings of the blood red as the rose
It sings of Majnun's heart which overflows.

And though the long road may be stained with blood
A fish will find its comfort in the flood.

The day is long for him who has no bread
So pass this day with wines of love instead.

To reach enlightenment though each must try,
This poem has to end—and so goodbye!

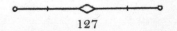

ON HIS DEATH

Bear my body to the grave my mortal friends
Knowing that the singing of my heart never ends

No time for your wailing, gnashing of teeth, and tears
The eternal sleep is not at all what it appears.

The grave is not the sum of a life complete
It is but the veil beyond which bride and groom
retreat.

You saw the body descending, now see it rise,
Think of me with Him as you shut your eyes

Locked in that coffin my soul is now set free
To join with my beloved in eternity.

Which seed fell in this earth and did not grow?
Your material shape is a drop in the heavenly flow

Of water which springs from That eternal source
Life, death, these illusions, must take their course.

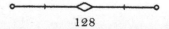

Is not the sun as it sinks, elsewhere rising too?
My grave is but the last door, the entrance to the
new.

So save your wails and mourning hymns for another
place
This flood bears me beyond, where man sees face to
face.

Translating Rumi

A Personal Note

Q & A with Farrukh Dhondy

A Personal Note

My great grandfather, Jamshedji Saklatwala, was something of a Persian scholar. One of the few things I know about him is that he used to spend his days attending the funerals of Parsi acquaintances in Bombay and sitting, as is the custom for males, outside the funeral parlor where prayers would be in session, translating Persian poetry in a small notebook. He published in his lifetime a book of translations into English of the *Rubaiyat of Omar Khayyam.* The family has the elaborately produced paperback, probably the only extant copy.

I read it years ago and found it very unexciting. In his preface, Jamshedji acknowledges the overbearing and irreplaceable presence of Edward Fitzgerald's beautiful and enduring translation of Khayyam's quatrains, but claims that he has set out to provide the reader with a more accurate translation.

The accuracy kills the poetry.

The Russian poet Yevgeny Yevtushenko remarked that "Translations are like women: if they are faithful, they are rarely beautiful; if they are beautiful, they are rarely faithful." His perception may today be labeled sexist, but whether the comparison is valid or not, one gets his drift.

I am, in this random selection of a few of Rumi's verses, setting out to do the opposite of what my great grandfather attempted to do with Khayyam. There is a craze in the United States for "Rumi" philosophy and verse, especially since Madonna (the American pop singer, not the Mother of Issah) reduced the medieval mystic to pop and recited his love songs. I have paid some attention to these lyrics and tried to read the translations on which they are based. My Persian is non-existent, but the verses in English, by several different translators, have succeeded in making Rumi's work a very unattractive proposition.

Rumi wrote his great work, the *Mathnawi*, in couplets. Though none of the translations I have read reproduce this form, I have attempted it in most cases and tried to imitate the meter of the original. The metaphor that Rumi uses is drawn, as is that of most Sufi poetry, from the landscape and usage of the time—the mirrors, the cups of wine that stand for the essence of the beloved, the lover who stands for the divine; the Word, the Book, the Messenger—these indicate the Koran and the Prophet Muhammad.

The way Rumi uses metaphor very often defies translation. There are ideas and concepts in the Persian language that merge, and in that merger provide lyrical sense. When translated into English they become disjointed ideas and monstrous images.

---

1. *Rumi Daylight, A Daybook of Spiritual Guidance*, translated by Camille and Kabir Helminski (Shambhalla South Asia Editions).

Everything is perishing except His face
Unless you have that Face, don't try to exist.[1]

These random lines from a huge outpouring of Rumi's translations demonstrate some of the difficulties. The translation has none of the grace of verse. ("Poetry" is in the eye, ear and sensibility of the beholder.) It resembles, more closely, an instruction in the manual of some modern electronic gadget manufactured in China. The translators may have attempted to capture something of the prose sense of Rumi's verse. "Everything perishing" becomes an abstraction in the translation. The argument about "having that Face" and the command to cease "trying to exist" if you don't are incomprehensible outside the context of Sufi discourse.

Rumi did not intend his verse to be read as we read haiku in contemporary translation—a random evocation and an illogical juxtaposition of images that can startle and perhaps make music but doesn't contain a sustained appeal to the eye, ear or any of the senses. In haiku, evocation is all, and none of the images in the translations I have read of Rumi are remotely evocative.

Take this, for instance:

There is some kiss we want with
Our whole lives, the touch of
Spirit on the body. Seawater
Begs the pearl to break its shell

And the lily, how passionately
It needs some wild darling!

                                        (Tr. Coleman Barks)

The metaphor of the kiss is confused by the abstraction
of wanting something with your "whole lives." The "touch
of the Spirit on body" is a further abstraction and the
image of the kiss that we were first given gets lost. Can
one want a kiss with a whole life? One may long for a
particular sort of kiss throughout one's life, or desire a
kiss with one's whole being, but the particular construction
above makes little logical or lyrical sense. Again, seawater
may erode the shell of the pearl, but can it really "beg"
it? Water wets, flows, rubs, erodes pebbles, pushes, drowns,
but can any of this appeal to our visual or tactile senses
as "begging"? It evokes no sensual response. And what
on earth is a "wild darling," outside the invented private
language of uninspired lovers who don't speak any known
English?

Another modern rendering distorts the meaning and,
perhaps for the sake of brevity, banishes any poetic intent:

Let lovers be crazy, disgraceful and wild
Those who fret about such things
Aren't in love.

                                        (Tr. Deepak Chopra)

The contention that wild abandon is the essence of love comes across, but the Sufi meaning of love doesn't. The translation is a fraud insofar as it pretends to be about adolescent romance and the "fretting" kills any lyrical flow.

There may be some virtue in translating poetry and seeking in the translation to convey the clumsiness and discomfort of reading a language that one doesn't know, but I have tried in my transliterations to do the opposite. It inevitably means taking liberties with the structure of the verses and sometimes altering the metaphor to get at what I think is the intended meaning.

For my money, the translations and commentaries of R. A. Nicholson, who translated and commented on Rumi from 1898 through the 1920s and '30s, remain the most faithful, erudite and comprehensively instructive. Professor A .J. Arberry of Pembroke College, Cambridge, translated the *Diwan-e Shams-e* in verse, attempting the rhyming couplets that are lyrically evocative and as faithful as translation can be. The fact that they are both British scholars of a particular age, "orientalists" in the contemptuous jargon of the more jargon-ridden modern academies, cannot detract from their achievement.

I confess that I am neither a Sufi nor a poet and, while working at these transliterations of Rumi, have used the texts of Nicholson and Arberry, the assistance and translating skills of friends who read Persian, and occasionally, the Urdu translations of Rumi by several scholars and commentators.

The liberties I have taken in trying to combine the intent of the original with an attempt at lyrical felicity are entirely mine and none other should beg forgiveness for them.

Q&A with
Farrukh Dhondy

Why did you decide to translate Rumi's works?

I was on a flight to Australia and for the first time was given a book of Rumi's verse in translation to read on the plane. I settled in to pass the hours in verse, having heard all my thinking life about Rumi but never having read anything. The verse was misnamed. All of it was prose, pretentiously broken into lines. It wasn't poetry, and it certainly wasn't Sufi in its content or conceit. On getting back to London, I looked for other versions. They all seemed to be written by New-Age spiritual freaks who took Rumi to be endorsing some mixed-metaphoric burden of wistful romance. All of them resembled either the fraudulent guides to happiness that are standard Californian fare, stumbling mis-understandings of simile and metaphor or very recondite and unintelligible constructions that refused to yield any meaning whatsoever.

Tomorrow is a hope—the dreamer's way

The Sufi lives the moment, rejoices in today!

139

HE KNOWS

"I know not what he knows, but I know he knows"

Thus the pupil fulfilled from the Master goes.

Why "A New Translation"?

I then discovered the earlier translations by Nicholson, which were in imitation eighteenth- or nineteenth-century English, but were meticulous and faithful to Rumi's metaphors, meanings and narratives. I had someone read me a few verses of the original Persian and then read some Urdu renderings of the *Mathnawi*. I paid attention to the meter and rhyme patterns, and thought I could do reasonable renderings of some of the verse. Here it is.

Why is Rumi's work gathering popularity and momentum today? And why has the West taken to him?

Since I started the work, I have found that there are several westerners who are convinced that they have Sufi inclinations. We live in an age of cults and new sectarian allegiances. Perhaps all ages suffered the same personal quests. In the USA, Rumi's following gathered momentum when some famous pop singers professed to be his followers. His popularity in other countries has certainly been given a boost by the growing curiosity towards non-violent Islam in the face of the outbreak of terrorist jihadism, which claims to be the true faith dedicated to secrecy and terror.

What was the experience like, translating works of Rumi? What were the difficulties in rendering the translation contemporary?
Rumi and the poets of the Sufi tradition are bound to a certain universe of imagery and expression without, if possible, sacrificing their individuality. The images of wine, the tavern, the beloved, of animals and their noted characteristics, the style of the parable, the attack on ritualized religious practice, the negation of the material to penetrate to the spirit are all parts of the convention. Finding the contemporary language and imagery in which to express these without violating or stepping outside that universe of discourse was the challenge. Rendering the verses in rhyme and iambic pentameter are

MATERIAL THE EARTH

Material is the earth and material the stars

O Rumi, seek the spirit—the water not the vase!

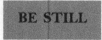

part of the craft without which the effect of verse, rather than discourse, cannot be sustained.

Is Rumi still relevant today? Where does he stand in the political and social upheaval that the Islamic world is going through?

The vast majority of Muslims in the world follow non-juridical Islam. The fundamentalist Wahabi strain and the political Islam, represented by the Egyptian-initiated Muslim Brotherhood, are antithetical to the tradition which Rumi preached and partly founded. There is no strain of political persuasion in his work. He distinctly renders that which is Caesar's which is his by ignoring it.

Ironically, the terrorist persuasion of those who claim to be evangelical Muslims has stimulated the quest for the lyrical, mystical, Sufi faith.

Be still as stone Refrain from speech And laughter

You shall be given A silken tongue In the world, hereafter.

What is the importance of the sufiana stream in the shaping of Islamic identity?

I do not believe that there is one

142

Islamic identity. That several peoples of the world are united by their belief in a faith by following its tenets doesn't give the followers of the nation of Islam in America the same identity as the Muslim in Jakarta or Srebrenica. Each section of the Umma is influenced by the society of which it is a part. Sufiana, though it is as old and older than Islam, has the potential to coexist without compromise with the modern world, unlike some strands of contemporary Islam.

Like Rumi, who are your other favorite poets?

I wouldn't claim that Rumi is my favorite poet. Shakespeare, Wordsworth, Keats, Tennyson, W. B. Yeats, T. S. Eliot are my lasting favorites, and some of my contemporaries, too many to mention, have alluring, individual and enlightening ways of putting the world to words.

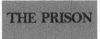

THE PRISON

When God has made the earth for you to roam

Why have you made a prison cell your home?

A great spiritual master and poet, **Jalal-ad-Din Rumi** was born in Wakhsh (Tajikistan) in 1207 to a family of learned theologians. He founded the Mawlawi Sufi order, a leading mystical brotherhood of Islam. He was initiated into the mystical path by a wandering dervish, Shamsuddin of Tabriz. His love for and his bereavement at the death of Shams found their expression in a surge of music, dance and lyric poems, *Divian-e Shams-e Tabrizi*. He is also the author of the six-volume epic work, the *Mathnawi*, which has been referred to as the "Koran in Persian."

Farrukh Dhondy was born in 1944 in Pune, India. After graduating in physics from Wadia College, he won a scholarship to Cambridge to train as a quantum physicist but ended up reading for a BA in English. He is the author of a number of books, including East End at Your Feet (1977), Poona Company (1980), Bombay Duck (1990), The Bikini Murders (2008), and Adultery and Other Stories (2011). He has also written screenplays for film and television, including Split Wide Open (1999) and The Rising: Ballad of Mangal Pandey (2005). His opera based on the Just So Stories by Rudyard Kipling opened in London in 2012.